Animals that Live in Shells

Words by Dean Morris

Raintree Childrens Books
Milwaukee • Toronto • Melbourne • London

Library of Congress Number: 77-7911

　　4 5 6 7 8 9 0 81 80

Printed and bound in the United States of America.

Library of Congress Cataloging in Publication Data

Morris, Dean.
　　Animals that live in shells.

　　(Read about)
　　Includes index.
　　SUMMARY: An introduction to the physical
characteristics and behavior patterns of various
species of mollusks and crustaceans.
　　1.　Mollusks — Juvenile literature.
2.　Arthropoda — Juvenile literature.　3.　Echino-
dermata — Juvenile literature.　4.　Shells — Juvenile
literature. [1.　Mollusks.　2.　Shells.
3.　Crustacea]　I.　Title.

QL405.2.M67　594　77-7911
ISBN 0-8393-0013-1 lib. bdg.

This book has been reviewed for accuracy by

Dr. David H. Stansbery
Director and Professor
The Ohio State University Museum of Zoology

Animals that Live in Shells

Many of the first animals lived in the sea. They had soft bodies. Some of these early animals developed hard shells or exoskeletons which protected their bodies. It was harder for other sea animals to eat them.

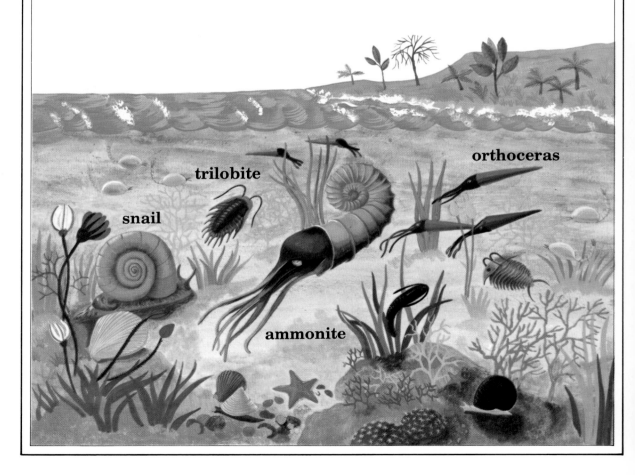

snail

trilobite

ammonite

orthoceras

When these animals died, their shells fell into the mud of the ocean floor. The mud became stone. Some shells became stone too. The shapes of some of these old shells can still be seen in rocks. These shells and shapes are called fossils. Fossils tell us how the first animals looked.

crab

prawn

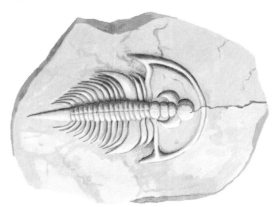

**trilobite
(extinct)**

**ammonite
(extinct)**

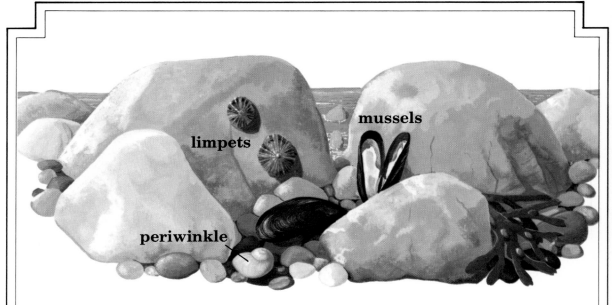

Many animals with shells live in the sea today. Some live on rocky beaches. When the tide comes in, water covers them. When it goes out, it leaves pools in the rocks where the animals live.

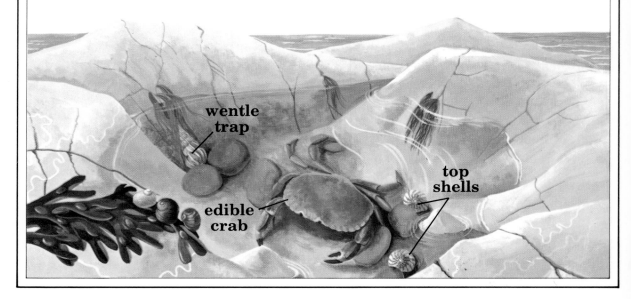

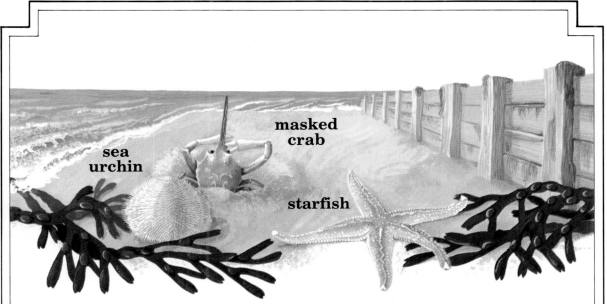

Other shelled animals live on sandy beaches. They dig themselves into the wet sand when the tide goes out. When the tide comes in, the animals may come out of their holes and feed.

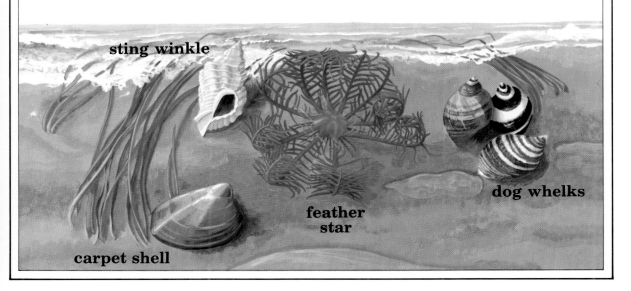

**giant
tortoises**

Some animals with shells live on land.
The giant tortoise moves very slowly. It
often has a very heavy shell. The tortoise's
shell protects it from its enemies. This
animal can pull its legs and head inside
its shell.

Some tortoises live for as long as
100 years.

Turtles, like tortoises, have shells.
Some turtles live in the sea. They spend
almost all of their time in the water.
These turtles usually leave the water only
when it is time to lay their eggs. The
eggs are laid in deep holes in the sand.
People used to hunt tortoises and turtles.
They made things out of the animals' shells.
Sometimes they used the animals for food.

green turtle

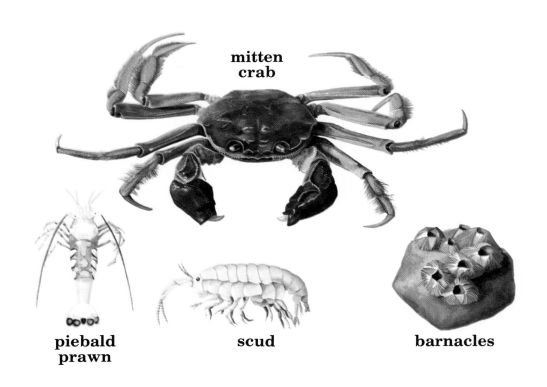

mitten crab

piebald prawn

scud

barnacles

Crustaceans are animals with jointed
exoskeletons or shells. A crustacean's
shell covers all of its body. It is like
a suit of armor. The parts of the shell fit
together in a way that lets the animal move.
Most crustaceans live in the water.

Crabs are crustaceans. Many different
kinds of crabs live along the seashore.

A hard shell covers a crab's body.
Shell also covers its eight walking legs
and its two pincers. Crabs can pick up
pieces of food with their pincers.

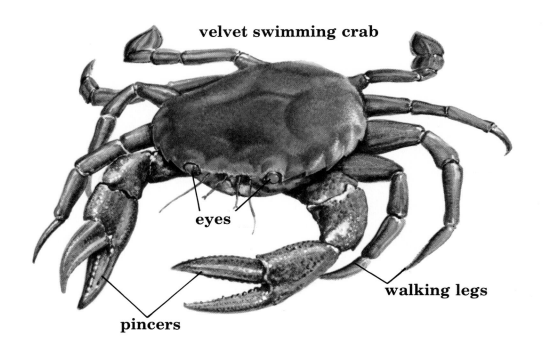

velvet swimming crab

eyes

pincers

walking legs

Crabs use their four pairs of walking legs to move along. They can easily walk sideways as well as forward and backward.

Some crabs have flat back legs that look like oars. These crabs are good swimmers.

Crabs can dig quickly. They can bury themselves in the sand.

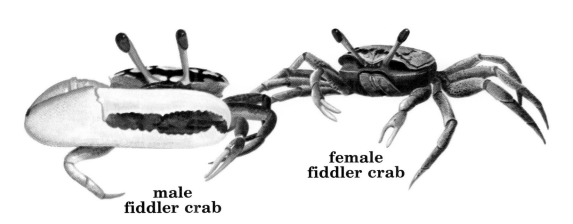

female
fiddler crab

male
fiddler crab

Fiddler crabs live in places that are warm. The male fiddler crab has one huge pincer. He waves the pincer and frightens away most other animals.

spider crab

Spider crabs have long, thin legs. If a predator comes near, the spider crab pulls in its legs and protects itself.

The hermit crab has a soft body. It has no hard shell of its own. It finds an empty snail shell and crawls in. Young hermit crabs live in small shells. They must find larger shells as they get bigger.

When disturbed, the hermit crab pulls its body into the shell. Its pincers block the shell's opening.

Lobsters are ocean animals too. Lobsters have jointed bodies with hard shell coverings. They have walking legs and pincers like other crustaceans. They use their huge pincers to catch food and to protect themselves.

The lobster grows. Soon it is too big for its first shell. It hides in a safe place. It wiggles out of the old hard shell. A new soft shell is underneath. The lobster grows rapidly before the shell gets hard. It does this again and again as it grows larger.

lobster

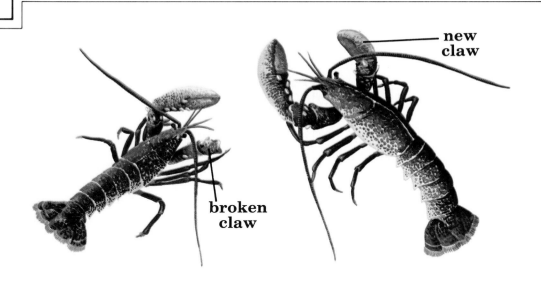

new
claw

broken
claw

Sometimes a lobster loses a claw. A new one may grow in its place.

Many people like to eat lobster meat. They use traps called pots to catch the lobsters. They lower the pots to the bottom of the sea. The lobsters can crawl into the pots, but they cannot crawl out.

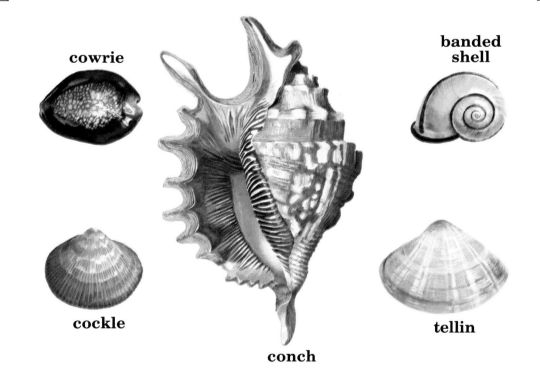

cowrie

banded shell

conch

cockle

tellin

Mollusks are soft-bodied animals.
Many have shells. Their hard shell coverings
protect their soft bodies.

Some mollusks have a one-piece shell.
Other mollusks have a shell of two pieces.
Others have a shell of eight pieces.
The mollusk shell may be inside or outside.
Some have no shell at all.

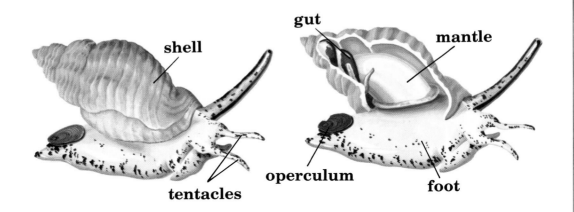

shell

gut

mantle

operculum

tentacles

foot

Whelks are snails that live inside coiled shells.

This kind of animal has a large, soft foot it uses to move. It carries its shell along with it.

When the animal is disturbed, it moves into its shell. The operculum closes the shell opening like a door. The animal is safer inside its shell.

The nautilus is another mollusk that has a one-piece shell. The shell has many closed spaces called chambers. As a new chamber is formed, the old one closes up. The animal lives in the chamber nearest the outside.

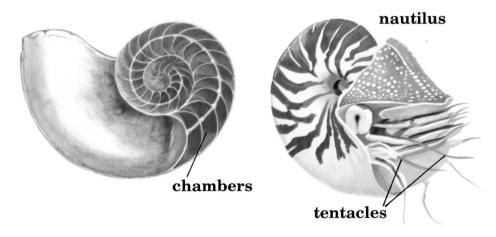

nautilus

chambers

tentacles

Each closed chamber is filled with gases. The gases help the nautilus float. The nautilus uses its strong tentacles to hold onto rocks. It can catch food with them too.

garden snails

Garden snails are mollusks that live on land. They like to eat plants.

A garden snail moves along on its foot. The foot leaves a trail of slime. The slime helps the snail to move along.

A snail has two pairs of antennae on its head. The large ones are for seeing. The small ones are for smelling.

Some snails live
in ponds in still
water. They find food
on plants that grow in
the ponds. Some lay
their eggs on the weeds.

**pouch
snail**

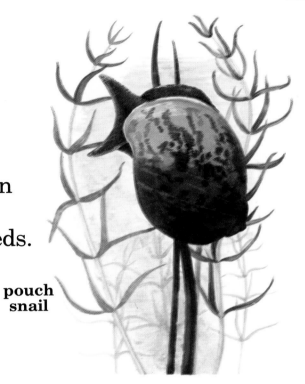

Some snails have
both male and female
parts.

These snails are
giving each other
sperm cells. Both
snails will be able
to lay eggs.

oyster

mussel

horse's hoof
clam

cockle

Mollusks that have a shell of two pieces are called bivalves. Valve is another word for half of the shell. Strong muscles close a bivalve's shell.

The animal's soft body may contract within the shell. It is protected there.

All bivalves live in the water. Bivalves draw water into their shells. Tiny pieces of food come in with the water. The bivalves may eat them.

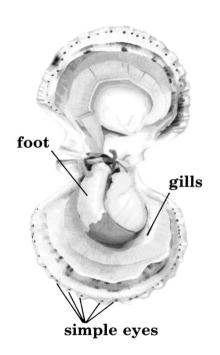

foot

gills

simple eyes

Scallops are bivalves that can swim. Not many bivalves can. The scallop moves by flapping its two valves together and squirting out water.

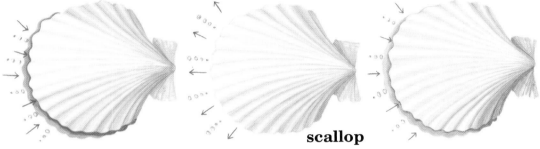

scallop

Mussels are bivalves that live on rocks. They make a liquid that turns hard. It forms a thread called a byssus. Mussels become fastened to the rocks with these threads. If a byssus breaks, the mussel can grow a new one.

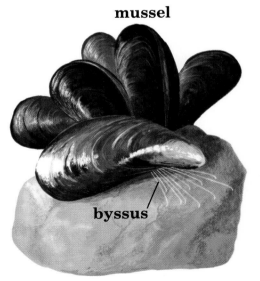

mussel

byssus

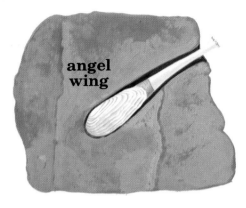

angel wing

Angel wings use their shells to bore holes into rocks. The shells have rows of tiny spines that can be used like a file.

Many other bivalves bury themselves too. They dig down into mud or sand. Bivalves need water to live. When they bury themselves, they push up tubes, called siphons. They move water in through one tube, remove oxygen from the water, then move the water out through the other tube.

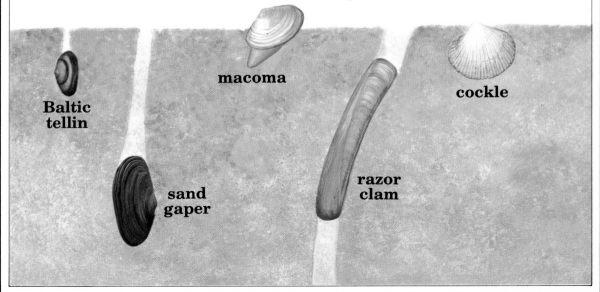

Baltic tellin

macoma

sand gaper

razor clam

cockle

This is how one bivalve buries itself.

The razor clam pushes its foot far down into the sand. The end of the foot expands, forming an anchor. Then the foot contracts, pulling the shell down into the sand.

When the animal moves up again, it sets its foot firmly outside the shell, expands the foot out and down, and pushes the shell up.

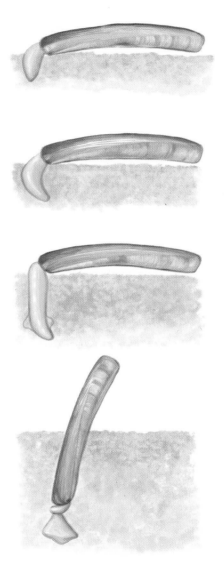

Giant squids are the biggest mollusks of all. The squid has no outer shell. Its shell is inside its body. The squid's long tentacles have suckers which catch other animals.

A squid passes water in through a tube, over the gills and then out. This causes the animal to move forward or backward. That is how it swims.

squids

The cuttlefish, like the squid, is a mollusk that has a shell inside its body. Cuttlefish bury themselves in the sand on the bottom of the sea.

cuttlefish

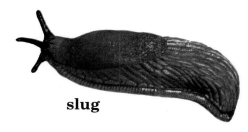

slug

The slug is a mollusk too. Some slugs have a small shell. Other slugs have no shell at all. Slugs live on land.

The octopus has no shell at all. It squirts out a thick ink when it is disturbed. The ink helps the octopus hide from enemies.

The octopus has eight long tentacles. It uses them to catch food.

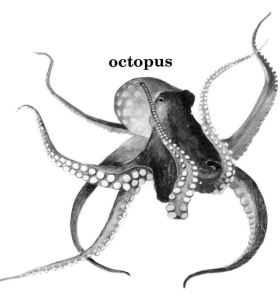

octopus

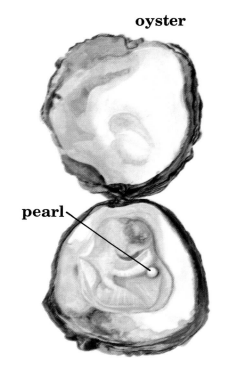

oyster

pearl

People use animals with shells in many ways.

The inside of some oyster shells is smooth and shiny. People use it to make many beautiful things.

Pearls are sometimes formed inside oyster shells. Pearls have great worth. Divers swim down to the ocean floor to look for them.

Some oysters are grown especially for
people to eat. They are farmed in spaces
called oyster beds. When the oysters are
fully grown, the farmer rakes them up.
Pearls are grown in a similar way too.

When shell animals die, the soft parts rot. Waves often wash the empty shells onto the beach. Each animal's shell has a different shape. Many shells have beautiful colors and markings.

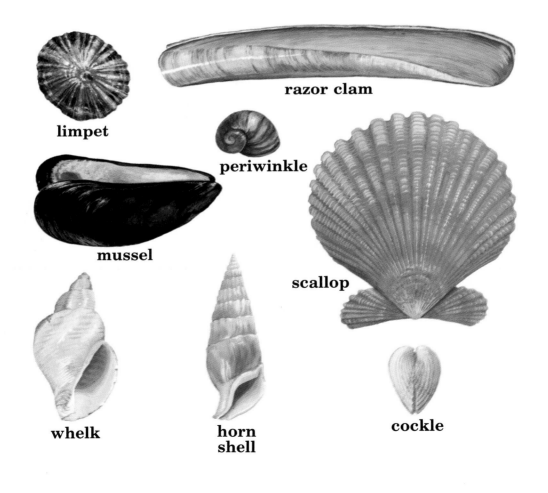

limpet

razor clam

periwinkle

mussel

scallop

whelk

horn shell

cockle

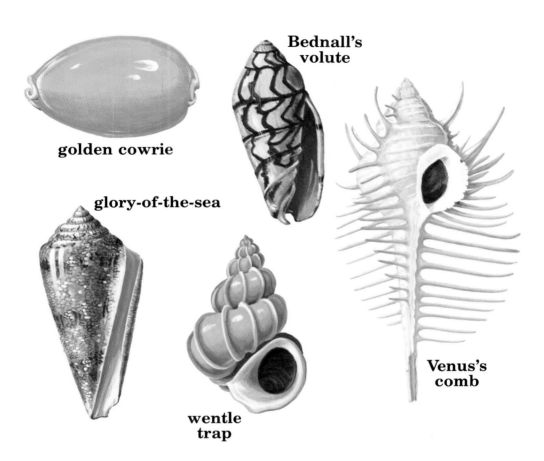

Bednall's volute

golden cowrie

glory-of-the-sea

Venus's comb

wentle trap

Some people collect sea shells. Many shells are easy to find. The shells on this page are rare. Only a few of them have ever been found.

Shells can be used to make music.
A conch shell can be blown like a horn.
A hole is made in the top of the shell.
Blowing through the hole makes a loud noise.
Aztecs used such horns in processions long ago.

In some parts of
the world, people use
shells as money.
People who live
on some Pacific Ocean
islands use cowrie
shells to buy food and
clothing.

money
cowrie

murex

When murex snails
are ground up, they
make a purple dye.
Long ago the Romans
learned how to use the
murex snails this way.
They wanted to color
cloth with the dye.
Important leaders wore
white clothing with
purple stripes.

Where to Read About the Animals that Live in Shells

green turtle (grēn turt′ əl) *p. 9*

hermit crab (hur′ mit krab) *p. 14*

horse's hoof clam (hôrs′ əs hoof klam)
  p. 22

limpet (lim′ pət) *pp. 6, 30*

lobster (lob′ stər) *pp. 15, 16*

macoma (mä cō mä) *p. 24*

masked crab (masked krab) *p. 7*

mitten crab (mit′ ən krab) *p. 10*

murex (myoo′ reks′) *p. 33*

mussel (mus′ əl) *pp. 6, 22, 23, 30*

nautilus (nô′ ti ləs) *p. 19*

octopus (ok′ tə pəs) *p. 27*

orthoceras (ôr thos′ ər əs) *p. 4*

oyster (ois′ tər) *pp. 22, 28, 29*

periwinkle (per′ ə wing′ kəl) *pp. 6, 30*

piebald prawn (pī′ bôld prôn) *p. 10*

pouch snail (pouch snāl) *p. 21*

prawn (prôn) *p. 5*

razor clam (rā′ zər klam) *pp. 24, 25, 30*

sand gaper (sand gā′ pər) *p. 24*

scallop (skol′ əp *or* skal′ əp) *pp. 23, 30*

scud (skəd) *p. 10*

sea urchin (sē ər′ chən) *p. 7*

Pronunciation Key for Glossary

a	a as in **cat**, **bad**
ā	a as in **able**, ai as in **train**, ay as in **play**
ä	a as in **father**, **car**
e	e as in **bend**, **yet**
ē	e as in **me**, ee as in **feel**, ea as in **beat**, ie as in **piece**, y as in **heavy**
i	i as in **in**, **pig**
ī	i as in **ice**, **time**, ie as in **tie**, y as in **my**
o	o as in **top**
ō	o as in **old**, oa as in **goat**, ow as in **slow**, oe as in **toe**
ô	o as in **cloth**, au as in **caught**, aw as in **paw**, a as in **all**
oo	oo as in **good**, u as in **put**
o͞o	oo as in **tool**, ue as in **blue**
oi	oi as in **oil**, oy as in **toy**
ou	ou as in **out**, ow as in **plow**
u	u as in **up**, **gun**, o as in **other**
ur	ur as in **fur**, er as in **person**, ir as in **bird**, or as in **work**
yo͞o	u as in **use**, ew as in **few**
ə	a as in **again**, e as in **broken**, i as in **pencil**, o as in **attention**, u as in **surprise**
ch	ch as in **such**
ng	ng as in **sing**
sh	sh as in **shell**, **wish**
th	th as in **three**, **bath**
<u>th</u>	th as in **that**, **together**

GLOSSARY

These words are defined the way they are used in this book.

anchor (ang′ kər) an object that holds something firmly in place

antenna (an ten′ ə) the long, thin movable part on the head of some animals used for seeing, smelling, or feeling

armor (är′ mər) a hard covering worn for protection

Aztec (az′ tek′) one of the group of people who founded the Mexican empire conquered by Cortes in 1519

backward (bak′ wərd) away from; to the rear; toward the back

beach (bēch) the land along the edge of a body of water

bivalve (bī′ valv′) an animal having two movable shells

blown (blōn) to make sounds by blowing air through

body (bod′ ē) the whole of a person, animal, or plant

bore (bôr) to make a hole by digging

bury (ber′ ē) to cover with earth or rock

byssus (bis′ əs) a thread made by some mollusks which fastens them to other things

chamber (chām′ bər) an enclosed space within the body or shell of a plant or animal

claw (klô) a sharp, curved nail on an animal's foot

coil (koil) something that is or appears to be wound round and round in a spiral

collect (kə lekt′) to gather together

contract (kən trakt′) to become smaller or shorter by pressing together

crustacean (krus tā′ shən) an animal that usually lives in water that has a hard shell or exoskeleton, two pair of antennae, and a divided body

develop (di vel′ əp) to grow and change

disturb (dis turb′) to break up or upset the state of rest or calm of a person or animal

diver (dī′ vər) someone who works or explores underwater

dye (dī) something that is used to give
   color to cloth, food, or other materials
especially (es pesh′ ə lē) more than usual
exoskeleton (ek′ sō skel′ ət ən) the
   hard, firm outer covering of some animals
expand (eks pand′) to become larger
fasten (fas′ ən) to put things together in
   a way that they cannot easily come apart
female (fē′ māl) the sex that produces eggs
   or gives birth to young
file (fīl) a metal tool with narrow cutting
   strips used to cut, smooth, or form a
   hard surface
firm (furm) not easily moved; fixed in place
flap (flap) to move up and down
float (flōt) to rest on top of, or within, air or
   water or to move slowly through air or water
form (fôrm) to take shape
forward (fôr′ wərd) to move ahead
fossil (fos′ əl) remains or traces of an
   animal or plant that lived many years ago
gas (gas) matter that is not solid or
   liquid and has no shape

gill (gil) the part of a fish and many other water animals used in breathing

grown (grōn) become as large as something is supposed to; adult in size

huge (hyōoj) very large; of great size

ink (ingk) a colored liquid usually used for writing, printing, or drawing; the black substance an octopus gives off from its body which protects it

itself (it self′) that same one

liquid (lik′ wid) a freely moving form of matter that is not a solid or a gas

lose (lōoz) to have no longer; to be without

male (māl) of the sex that produces sperm cells

muscle (mus′ əl) organs which move animal skeletons by contracting

oar (ôr) a long pole that is wide at one end and is used to move a boat in the water

onto (ôn′ tōo *or* on′ tōo) to a place on or above

operculum (ō pər′ kyə ləm) the part of some snails that closes the shell when the animal is inside

oxygen (ok′ sə jən) a gas with no color or smell that people, plants, and animals must have to live

pearl (purl) a small, round object formed inside some mollusks and used as a gem

pincer (pin′ chər) a kind of claw on some animals used to pick up food, hold things, or dig

pool (pōol) a small body of water

predator (pred′ ə tər) an animal that lives by hunting other animals for food

procession (prə sesh′ ən) a group of people who are moving forward in a special order

purple (pur′ pəl) the color made by mixing red and blue

rake (rāk) to gather things together using a tool with a long handle with teeth attached to one end

rapidly (rap′ id lē) very quickly

rare (rer) something not often seen, found, or happening

remove (ri mōov′) to take or move something away

rot (rot) the wasting away of animal or
   plant matter
sandy (san′ dē) made of or like sand
seashore (sē′ shôr′) land near or on
   the sea
shiny (shīn′ nē) bright; filled with light
sideways (sīd′ wāz′) a movement to or from
   the side
similar (sim′ əl ər) to be alike or much
   the same
siphon (sī′ fən) a part in some animals,
   shaped like a tube, that carries liquids in
   and out of the body
slime (slīm) a slippery substance that is
   thick like jelly
smooth (smooth) not rough; even or level
space (spās) all the room within an area
sperm cell (spurm sel) the male part of
   the process by which living things make
   others like themselves
spine (spīn) something sharp and pointed
   that may grow on some plants
   or animals

squirt (skwurt) to force out liquid in a
   narrow stream through a small opening
sucker (suk′ ər) a round, disclike part
   of an animal's body that lets it hold
   onto something
tentacle (ten′ tə kəl) the long, thin,
   movable part of some animals used to
   feel, hold, or help them move
themselves (t͟hem selvz′ *or* t͟həm selvz′)
   the same ones
thread (thred) a long, thin cord
tide (tīd) the usual rise and fall of
   large bodies of water caused by the gravity
   pull of the sun and moon
tube (to͞ob *or* tyo͞ob) a hollow piece of
   material shaped like a pipe
underneath (un′ dər nēth′) under or below
   something
valve (valv) the movable shell of some animals
weed (wēd) a plant that grows where
   it is not wanted by people; a plant
   that is so common that people do
   not value it

wiggle (wig′ əl) to make short, quick movements from side to side

within (wi<u>th</u> in′ *or* with in′) in or into the inside of

Bibliography

Burton, Maurice, and Burton, Robert, editors. *The International Wildlife Encyclopedia.* 20 vols. Milwaukee: Purnell Reference Books, 1970.

Russell, Solveig Paulson. *The Crusty Ones: A First Look at Crustaceans.* New York: Henry Z. Walck, 1974.
Surveys the class of animals called crustaceans describing their characteristics, habitats, structure, development, and importance in the food cycle.

Schisgall, Oscar. *That Remarkable Creature, the Snail.* New York: Julian Messner, 1970.
Describes the habits of the more common land, freshwater, and sea snails.

Trent, Robbie. *Shells from the Sea.* Waco, Tex.: Word Books, 1975.

Wong, Herbert H., and Vessel, Matthew F. *My Snail.* Reading, Mass.: Addison-Wesley Publishing Company, 1976.

Zim, Herbert Spencer, and Krantz, Lucretia. *Snails.* New York: William Morrow & Company, 1975.
A general introduction to gastropods, or snails, of which there are approximately 80,000 kinds living in the sea, in fresh water, and on land.